Life in a Castle

Kay Eastwood

 Crabtree Publishing Company

www.crabtreebooks.com

Crabtree Publishing Company

www.crabtreebooks.com

Coordinating editor: Ellen Rodger

Series editor: Carrie Gleason

Designer and production coordinator: Rosie Gowsell

Scanning technician: Arlene Arch-Wilson

Art director: Rob MacGregor

Project development, editing, photo editing, and layout:

First Folio Resource Group, Inc.: Erinn Banting, Molly Bennett, Tom Dart, Jaimie Nathan, Debbie Smith, Anikó Szöcs

Photo research: Maria DeCambra

Research: Tara Steele

Consultants: Joseph Goering, Department of History, University of Toronto; Linda Northrup, Department of Near and Middle Eastern Civilizations, University of Toronto; David Waterhouse, Professor Emeritus of East Asian Studies, University of Toronto

Photographs: Paul Almasy/Corbis/Magma: p. 13 (bottom); Archivo Iconografico, S.A./Corbis/Magma: p. 22, pp. 28–29; Art Archive: p. 19; Art Archive/Biblioteca Estense Modena/Dagli Orti: p. 25 (top); Art Archive/Bibliothèque Municipale Rouen/Dagli Orti: title page; Art Archive/Bodleian Library Oxford/Bodley 264 folio 228: cover; Art Archive/Bodleian Library Oxford/Canon liturg. 99 folio 16r: p. 21; Art Archive/British Library: p. 26; Art Archive/Dagli Orti: p. 12 (bottom); Art Archive/University Library Prague/Dagli Orti: p. 25 (bottom); Yann Arthus-Bertrand/Corbis/Magma: p. 31 (top); John Bethell/ Bridgeman Art Library: p. 8 (bottom left); Bodleian Library, University of Oxford/MS Douce 5 f.7: p. 20 (bottom); John Elk III/Elk Photography: p. 17; Mary Evans Picture Library: p. 13 (top), p. 18, p. 24 (bottom); Fitzwilliam Museum, University of Cambridge, UK/Bridgeman Art Library: p. 27 (top); Giraudon/ Art Resource, NY: p. 5 (bottom), p. 12 (top); Jason Hawkes/ Corbis/Magma: p. 7 (bottom); Doranne Jacobson: p. 30 (left); © Simon Lewis 2003: p. 8 (top left); Gianni Dagli Orti/Corbis/ Magma: p. 7 (top); Royalty-Free/Corbis/Magma: p. 30 (right); Scala/Art Resource, NY: p. 23 (bottom); Snark/Art Resource, NY: p. 24 (top); Sandro Vannini/Corbis/Magma: p. 8 (bottom right); Adam Woolfitt/Corbis/Magma: p. 8 (top right), p. 27 (bottom), p. 31 (bottom)

Illustrations: Jeff Crosby: p. 6; Gary Cross: pp. 10–11, p. 16; Katherine Kantor: title page (border), copyright page (bottom), p. 4 (feudal pyramid), p. 7 (box), p. 14 (top, left), p. 15 (top left, bottom), p. 17 (banner), p. 19 (banner); Margaret Amy Reiach: title page (illuminated letter), copyright page (top), contents page (all), p. 4 (timeline, feudal pyramid, border), p. 5 (map), p. 9, p. 11 (gold boxes), p. 14 (bottom right), p. 15 (top right), p. 20 (center), p. 23 (top), p. 32 (all)

Cover: Medieval castles were very busy places.

Title page: Castles had a Great Hall, which was a large room used for feasting, dancing, and meetings with other lords and tenants who lived on castle lands.

Crabtree Publishing Company

www.crabtreebooks.com   1-800-387-7650

Cataloging-in-Publication Data
Eastwood, Kay.
　Life in a castle / written by Kay Eastwood.
　　p. cm. -- (Medieval world series)
Includes index.
Summary: Describes different kinds of castles, their purposes, how they were built, and what it was like to live in a castle, looking particularly at the roles played by women and children.
　ISBN 0-7787-1343-1 (RLB) -- ISBN 0-7787-1375-X (pbk)
　1. Castles--Juvenile literature. 2. Civilization, Medieval--Juvenile literature. [1. Castles. 2. Civilization, Medieval.] I. Title. II. Series.
　GT3550.E27 2003
　728.8'1--dc22
　　　　　　　　　　　　　　　2003016188
　　　　　　　　　　　　　　　　　LC

Published in the United States
PMB 16A
350 Fifth Ave.,
Suite 3308
New York, NY
10118

Published in Canada
616 Welland Ave.,
St. Catharines,
Ontario, Canada
L2M 5V6

Published in the United Kingdom
73 Lime Walk,
Headington,
Oxford
OX3 7AD
United Kingdom

Published in Australia
386 Mt. Alexander Rd.,
Ascot Vale (Melbourne)
V1C 3032

Table of Contents

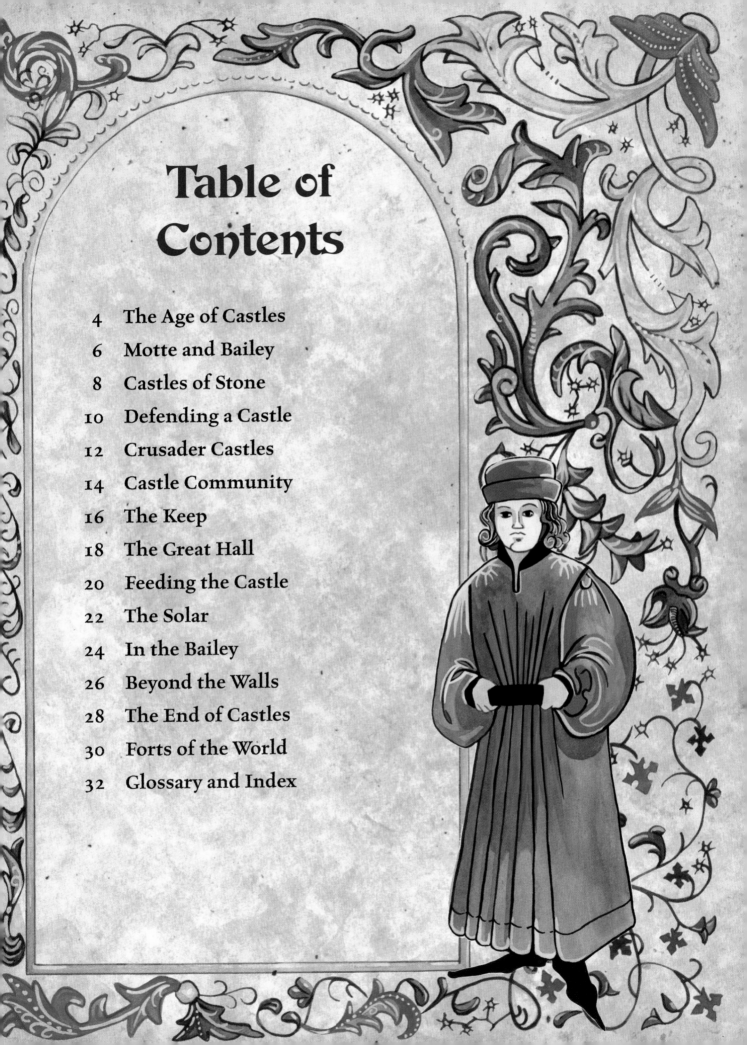

The Age of Castles

The Middle Ages is a period of history that stretched from 500 A.D. to 1500 A.D. During this time, people in western Europe lived under a system called feudalism.

The most powerful people in a feudal society were nobles, such as kings and great lords, who owned large areas of land. To keep control over their territory and defend it from enemies, they gave **lesser nobles** who supported them, called vassals, sections of land, called fiefs.

The vassals gave smaller pieces of land, called manors, to warriors who fought on horseback. These warriors, called knights, promised to fight for their lords for 40 days a year.

▶ *Most people in the Middle Ages were peasants. Power, wealth, and land was in the hands of very few nobles.*

▶ King

▶ Great lords

▶ Lesser nobles

▶ Knights

▶ Peasants

Viking attacks begin **800**	**Norman conquerors build many wooden castles in England** **1066**	**Shell keeps and square keeps become common** **1100**	**Peak of castle design and construction in Europe. Feudalism declines** **1300**
850 First motte and bailey castles built	**1097** Tower of London completed in stone	**1150** Crusaders returning from Holy Land introduce new ideas in castle design	**1347** Black Death strikes Europe, killing more than one third of the population

Fighting for Power

Kings, lords, and knights constantly fought each other for land and power. At the same time, parts of Europe were being attacked by outside **invaders**. To defend themselves and their families, nobles built **fortified** homes called castles.

From the castle, nobles looked after their manors, collected **taxes** from the peasants who lived on their land, solved arguments between villagers, and acted as judges in courts of law. Kings and lords often had more than one castle, which they visited throughout the year.

Castles Outside Europe

People outside Europe, in places such as Japan, India, and Egypt, also built large, strong forts to defend themselves against enemies. Some of these forts were also homes, like European castles.

▲ Peasants who lived in small villages on a manor farmed the lord's land in return for the lord's protection and small fields on which to raise crops for their families.

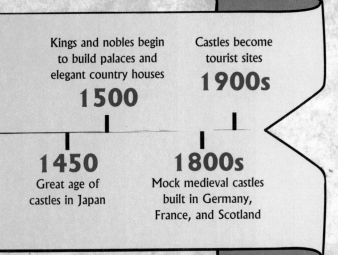

Kings and nobles begin to build palaces and elegant country houses
1500

Castles become tourist sites
1900s

1450
Great age of castles in Japan

1800s
Mock medieval castles built in Germany, France, and Scotland

Motte and Bailey

Location was very important to a castle's defense. Nobles had their castles built near the borders of their land or near roads and rivers they wanted to defend. By building castles on hilltops or mountain ridges, residents could see enemies approaching from far away. Castles on hills were also more difficult to attack.

Castles were built near rivers or lakes so the people who lived in them had water for drinking, washing, and filling the **moat**. Building a castle near a forest provided deer, boar, bears, and other **game** for nobles to hunt. The forest's wood was used for building, cooking, and heating the castle.

The earliest medieval castles were wooden motte and bailey castles built in the 800s. A motte was a flat-topped hill or mound of earth. On top of the motte was a simple wooden tower called a keep. The keep was both a watchtower and house for a lord's family. A palisade, or fence, of sharp wooden stakes surrounded the keep.

▶ *Even before nobles built castles in western Europe, Romans, who ruled the area until the 400s, built forts to defend their land. Housesteads Fort, in northern England, was built near a stream which provided constant running water.*

6

Building a Motte

If there was not a suitable hill on a lord's land, peasants built the motte by hand out of layers of earth and stone. Around the motte was a ditch or moat filled with water or sticks to keep the enemy away. Peasants build a motte in

this scene from the Bayeux Tapestry, a very long piece of material embroidered to celebrate the victory of William the Conqueror over the English in 1066. William was from Normandy, in present-day France. He fought Harold, the king of England, and took over all his land. Then, he built many motte and bailey castles to keep control of his new kingdom.

The Bailey

At the base of the motte was a large flat yard called a bailey. Inside the bailey were stables for horses, sheds and pens for livestock, storerooms for food, workshops, simple houses for servants, and buildings where soldiers slept. Another palisade and deep ditch surrounded the bailey. When attacked by another noble's army, local peasants went to the bailey with their livestock. If the enemy got past the bailey's palisade, the castle community retreated to the keep, high on its hill.

Castles of Stone

Around the year 1100, nobles began to build castles from stone instead of wood. Stone did not rot in damp weather like wood, and it provided better protection from an enemy's weapons.

◀ Shell Keeps

Some nobles made their motte and bailey castles stronger by building a stone wall around the motte instead of using a wooden palisade. Restormel Castle in England is an example of this type of castle, called a shell keep. The wooden buildings that once stood inside the wall rotted away long ago.

Collapsing Mottes ▶

Some stone keeps were built on top of mottes, but most mottes could not support the stone keep's enormous weight. As the motte began to collapse, the walls of some keeps cracked, as at Clifford's Tower in the city of York, in England.

◀ Square Keeps

Most nobles built new stone keeps in the bailey or at an entirely new location. These keeps, called square keeps or donjons, were usually tall, rectangular towers with very thick walls and tiny windows. Square keeps, such as the one at Rochester Castle in England, had watchtowers at their corners.

Concentric Castles ▶

Starting around 1250, lords protected their square keeps with strong stone walls called curtain walls. These walls provided better protection against new types of warfare. Concentric castles, such as Edinburgh Castle, in Scotland, had two or more curtain walls for even better defense. The only way to enter the castle was through a gatehouse in the outer wall. Gatehouses replaced the keep as the strongest place in the castle.

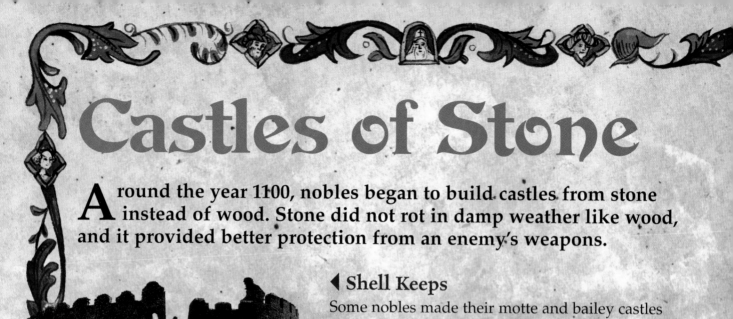

Building a Stone Castle

Stone castles were stronger than wooden castles, but took many years to build, were much more expensive because the stone had to be brought from far away, and required the labor of hundreds of workers. Most of the workers were peasants who were paid very little. Masons, who were skilled stone workers, were better paid. A highly skilled master mason supervised construction. He **surveyed** the site, drew up plans, arranged for materials to be brought to the site, hired workers, and gave them instructions.

Masons had only the simplest tools to build castles. They pulled stones up ramps with ropes or raised the stones with pulleys. To make sure a wall was perfectly straight, a mason hung a lead weight on a cord from the top of the wall. This was called a plumb line. If the weight touched the wall anywhere, it meant the wall was not straight.

Many other people helped build the castle. Miners dug the ditches for the castle's **foundations** and moat. **Plumbers** and tilers made roofs. Smiths made tools, nails, doors, and locks. Carpenters cut down trees and trimmed them into planks of wood for floors.

Defending a Castle

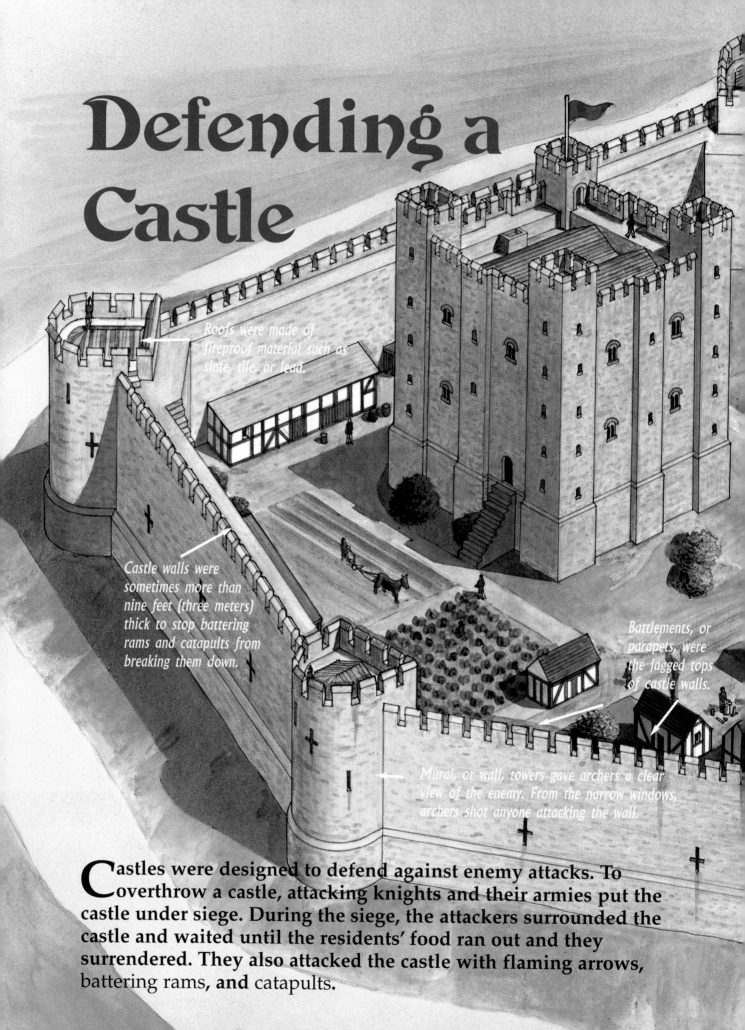

Roofs were made of fireproof material such as slate, tile, or lead.

Castle walls were sometimes more than nine feet (three meters) thick to stop battering rams and catapults from breaking them down.

Battlements, or parapets, were the jagged tops of castle walls.

Mural, or wall, towers gave archers a clear view of the enemy. From the narrow windows, archers shot anyone attacking the wall.

Castles were designed to defend against enemy attacks. To overthrow a castle, attacking knights and their armies put the castle under siege. During the siege, the attackers surrounded the castle and waited until the residents' food ran out and they surrendered. They also attacked the castle with flaming arrows, battering rams, **and** catapults.

Defenders fired longbows and crossbows from crenels.

The moat was filled with mud, water, or sticks.

Guards kept lookout from a wall walk.

Merlons protected defenders while they rested or reloaded.

Hoardings were temporary wooden walkways.

Defenders fired arrows through arrow loops.

Round towers did not have corners that blocked a defender's view.

Defenders used chains to pull up the drawbridge.

The heavy portcullis was lowered to keep the enemy out.

The gatehouse was the only way to enter the castle.

Splayed walls were thicker at the bottom than the top.

Crusader Castles

Many parts of a castle that improved its defense came from castles that Christian **warriors**, called crusaders, saw while fighting in the Holy Land. The Holy Land is an area east of the Mediterranean Sea that has special religious meaning for Christians, Muslims, and Jews. It includes modern-day Israel, Jordan, Syria, and Lebanon.

In the Holy Land, the crusaders saw **Byzantine** and Muslim castles with concentric walls, splayed walls, mural towers, and **machicolations**. When they returned to Europe, they built castles that looked like the ones in the Holy Land. Crusaders who stayed in the Holy Land after the fighting ended also built castles there to defend their newly conquered land.

▲ *Crusaders traveled from Europe to the Holy Land by foot, on horseback, and sometimes on ships. It took years to get there.*

▼ *Krak des Chevaliers, in present-day Syria, was originally a Muslim fortress. The crusaders captured it in 1109 and made it stronger by building mural towers and concentric walls. Krak des Chevaliers was so large that it could hold 6,000 soldiers and their horses.*

The Crusades

From 1095 to 1291, Christian warriors from Europe answered a call by Pope Urban II to retake the Holy Land from Muslims who had controlled the area since the 600s. Christians did not approve of Muslims' beliefs and they wanted the land for themselves. Pope Urban II promised that anyone who died fighting these holy wars, called crusades, would be forgiven for their sins and would go to heaven after they died. Kings, nobles, and knights, as well as peasants, left their homes and made the dangerous and expensive journey to free the area from the Muslims.

▼ *In 1197, England's King Richard the Lionheart built Chateau Gaillard in France to defend the land he conquered from the French king. The castle's concentric walls and moats were based on ones the king saw during the crusades.*

Castle Community

Castles were noisy, busy places in peacetime as well as in times of war. As many as 500 people lived in a castle when the lord and lady were home.

The Lady ▶

The main duty of the lord's wife, who was called a lady, was to have many children. The lady also ran the castle. She made sure supplies were ordered and bills were paid, and she supervised the servants. When the lady was not busy with these activities, she **embroidered**, played board games, talked with her ladies-in-waiting, and read books.

◀ The Lord

The lord fought for the noble who gave him land. He also looked after his manor and the people on it. In his spare time, the lord hunted wild game, practiced his fighting skills in pretend battles called tournaments, and played chess and other games.

◀ Pages and Squires

Pages and squires were noble boys sent to another lord's castle to learn how to become knights. They were taught to carve meat, serve food at the lord's table, use swords and other weapons, and ride a horse. They also went with their lord into battle.

Ladies-in-Waiting ▶

Ladies-in-waiting were girls from noble families who were sent to another noble's castle, where they learned to be ladies. They kept the lady of the castle company while they were taught how to run a castle, sew, embroider, sing, and dance.

▼ *In return for protecting the castle, knights without manors received a horse, food, and place to sleep within the castle walls. When the knights were not fighting, they trained in the bailey, played chess, and talked with the ladies of the castle.*

A Castle's Servants

A whole team of servants ran the castle. For example, in the kitchen there was a cook, a baker, a brewer who brewed beer, and a vintner who made wine. A pantler bought and stored the kitchen supplies, and scullions cleaned up the mess when the cooking was done. There was even a taster who tested the lord's food to make sure that it was not poisoned. These servants followed the lord and lady when they visited their other castles.

Only a few servants always stayed at the castle. The constable, or warden, looked after the castle when the lord and lady were away. He was also in charge of the **garrison** and the rest of the servants when the lord and lady were home. The steward, or seneschal, helped the constable supervise the castle. He also acted as a judge for minor crimes when the lord was busy or away.

▲ *Every castle had a chapel for saying prayers. The chaplain was a priest who led the prayers. He also advised the lord, read to the household in the evenings, and taught the lord's children to read.*

◄ *Nurses looked after young children.*

The Keep

The keep was the main building in early castles. It was both a home and a place where people went for safety during war. Later, when the gatehouse became the castle's main point of defense, the keep was mainly a home for the lord's family and servants.

Rooks in a Keep

① The solar was the lord and lady's private chamber.

② Large tanks, called cisterns, collected rainwater. Lead pipes carried the rainwater to lower floors.

③ Most prisoners waiting for trial in dungeons had to pay for their food. Some hung buckets from their cell windows to beg for donations from people passing by.

④ The Great Hall was the center of life in the castle.

⑤ Storerooms were filled with food, wine, and wood for fires. In times of war, when there were many knights at the castle, they slept in the storerooms.

⑥ The chapel was a place of prayer. Some chapels were two stories high. The lord's family sat in the upper story, which they entered through the solar, while the servants sat in the lower story, which they entered from the Great Hall.

⑦ The keep's entrance was often on the second floor to make it more difficult for enemies to enter.

⑧ Weapons and suits of armor were kept in the armory.

Dungeons

In the Middle Ages, people accused of crimes were held in dungeons. The dungeons were usually high up in the keep, so the accused could not escape. If prisoners were found guilty, they were usually fined, punished, or killed rather than being kept in dungeons.

Wealthy knights captured during battles were held in dungeons until their family or friends paid a large sum of money called a ransom. Raising a ransom often took years, especially for a king's ransom. Noble prisoners were usually treated like guests of the castle. It was important to keep them happy and healthy or the ransom would not be paid.

▲ Prisoners were kept inside a tower at the castle of Loches, in France.

The Great Hall

The most important room in the castle was the Great Hall. This enormous room was the only room in early castles. The lord, his family, and his servants ate, slept, and entertained themselves there. The lord also managed his manor from the Great Hall.

In later castles, the Great Hall was often a separate building. By this time, the lord and his family had private rooms, but some servants still slept in the Great Hall.

Dining in the Great Hall

The main meal of the day was served in late morning. It sometimes lasted two to three hours. People were seated in the Great Hall according to their importance. The lord, lady, and their special guests ate at one end of the Great Hall, at a raised table called a dais. They were the only diners to have chairs. The other diners sat on benches at the "low" tables. The tables were wooden planks set on **trestles** that were taken apart and stored between meals.

Plates and Cutlery

Very wealthy nobles ate from plates, but meals were usually served on pieces of stale bread, called trenchers. After the meal, the **almoner** gave the trenchers to the poor or fed them to the dogs.

It was common for people sitting next to each other to share a trencher and cup. Most places in Europe did not have forks yet, so people ate with their fingers, a knife, and sometimes a spoon. Diners washed their hands before and after dinner using water brought to the table in fancy jugs called ewers.

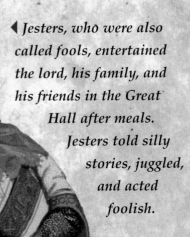

Jesters, who were also called fools, entertained the lord, his family, and his friends in the Great Hall after meals. Jesters told silly stories, juggled, and acted foolish.

Mealtime Behavior

Books about manners taught nobles how to behave at meals.

- Wash your hands before and after meals.
- Do not drink from your neighbor's cup if your mouth is full.
- Do not slurp your soup.
- Do not use your fingers to blow your nose.
- Do not pick your teeth with a knife while at the table.
- Do not blow on your food to cool it.
- Do not wipe your mouth on the tablecloth.
- If you are sharing a dish, do not leave your spoon in it.
- It is rude to belch or spit while at the table.
- You must never pass gas at the table.
- Do not put your fingers in your ears or scratch your head or any other part of your body while eating.
- Do not gnaw or suck on bones and return them to the dish.
- Do not pick out the best bits and eat them yourself.

Fun in the Great Hall

After the meal, the nobles danced and played games such as chess or backgammon. Often, everyone gathered to watch **minstrels**, acrobats, jugglers, jesters, and poets, or to listen to the chaplain read religious stories and stories about knights and ladies.

Feeding the Castle

Most of the food for the castle community came from the surrounding land, which nobles owned and peasants farmed. Fruit was grown in orchards and vineyards, and vegetables were grown in fields. There were also grazing areas for sheep, cattle, and goats, and fields that grew hay for animals to eat in the winter.

Food Fit for a Noble

Nobles ate vegetables, fruit, bread made from wheat, and a lot of fish and meat, including beef, **mutton**, pork, deer, rabbit, and goat. They also ate wild game, which they hunted on horseback with the help of their dogs. Nobles flavored their food with vinegar, wine, and herbs grown in the castle garden. Wealthy nobles could also afford spices such as pepper, cumin, cinnamon, and cloves, which they bought from **merchants** at fairs and markets.

▲ *Husbands and wives worked together in the fields.*

In the winter, when fresh food was scarce, nobles ate meat and fish that had been covered in salt or dried out over a fire. Salting and drying food helped keep it from going bad in the winter. Fruit and vegetables were also **preserved**.

▶ *Pigs were butchered in the fall and made into sausages.*

▲ *Bakers made loaves of bread in dome-shaped ovens heated by wood. They used long wooden shovels, called peels, to put the loaves in the oven and take them out. Bakehouses were usually in the bailey, away from the keep, in case of fire.*

Servants' Food

Servants and peasants ate simpler meals than nobles did. Servants ate what was left over in the castle kitchen, while peasants ate dark, coarse bread made from wheat mixed with rye or oatmeal, vegetables, and maybe a bit of pork. They sometimes also ate chicken, eggs, and cheese. A porridge-like dish called pottage was made from whatever ingredients were available, such as oats and vegetables flavored with bacon fat.

Washing it Down

The lord, lady, and their noble guests usually drank wine with their meals. Everyone else, including children, drank **ale**. Mead, a drink made from **fermented** honey, was also popular.

Feasts

Wealthy lords held great feasts to celebrate the birth of their children, their children's marriages, visits from important guests, and holidays. Extra courses were served, with unusual dishes such as swans and peacocks. These birds had their skins removed, then they were stuffed with spices and herbs, roasted, and sewn back into their feathers. After each course, diners ate fancy sweets made from almond paste and sugar brought from the **Middle East**. The sweets were shaped like castles, swans, and ships.

The Solar

In the earliest castles, the noble family slept at one end of the Great Hall. A curtain or screen usually separated their sleeping area from the rest of the hall. By 1100, the lord, lady, and their children had a private room. This room was called a solar, or a bower if it did not have windows.

Furniture

Like all rooms in a medieval castle, the lord and lady's private chamber had very little furniture. There were carved wooden chests to store clothes and sometimes a stool or bench to sit on. A fireplace helped keep the lord and lady warm.

The most valuable piece of furniture in the castle was the lord and lady's large four-poster bed. The bed had a feather mattress, pillows, sheets, quilts, and fur blankets to keep the lord and lady warm. For privacy, and to protect the lord and lady from drafts, the bed was surrounded with curtains that were pulled back during the day and closed at night. A canopy kept dust and insects from falling on the lord and lady as they slept.

▶ *All the furniture in the lord and lady's chamber, including the bed, was easily packed up and taken to their other castles.*

The Garderobe

In the Middle Ages, toilets were commonly called garderobes, from the French words *garder*, which means "look after," and *robes*, which means "clothes." Nobles stored their best clothes near the toilet because they thought the smell kept fleas away from their clothes.

Garderobes were often just little stone rooms that stuck out from a keep's wall. The toilet was usually a hole cut into a piece of stone, covered by a wooden seat. There was no such thing as toilet paper in the Middle Ages. People used handfuls of hay, straw, or torn strips of cloth. Waste emptied into a pit underneath the castle called a gong pit, into the moat, or into the base of the castle's walls. A gong farmer cleaned up the mess.

Taking a Bath

Lords and ladies bathed in a wooden tub shaped like a barrel. The tub had a wooden seat and sides that were padded with cloth for comfort. In cold weather, the tub was placed in the lord and lady's chamber near the fire. The water was heated in the kitchen and carried to the lord and lady's room, where servants poured it over the bather. In warm weather, the tub was often placed in the garden.

In the Bailey

A castle's bailey, or courtyard, was always full of activity.

In the bailey was a well, a laundry area, a mill to grind flour, ovens in which to bake bread, and a place to brew beer. There were also workshops for the weavers and tailors who made clothing for everyone in the castle, and for blacksmiths, coopers, and chandelers. Blacksmiths made almost everything metal in the castle, except for weapons and armor, which the armorer made. Coopers made the barrels in which vintners stored wine, and in which people bathed and washed their clothes. Chandelers made candles. A large household could burn 1,300 candles in a single winter's night!

The stables were in the bailey too. A stable marshal supervised the servants and grooms who took care of the horses, dogs, and falcons that the lord and lady used for hunting. Pigs, cows, goats, and chickens were kept in sheds and pens.

▲ *Tailors working in the bailey cut out and sewed clothing for castle residents.*

▶ *Blacksmiths often had a workshop in the bailey, where they shaped hot metal into horseshoes and tools.*

Coopers ▶

Coopers worked in the bailey, bending strips of wood and metal to make barrels. The barrels stored food, beer, and wine for the castle community.

▼ Markets

Weekly markets were held in the bailey, where peasants and traveling merchants traded their goods. There were stalls full of cheese, eggs, knives, shoes, cloth, and livestock. Vendors also wandered around the market, selling their goods from baskets.

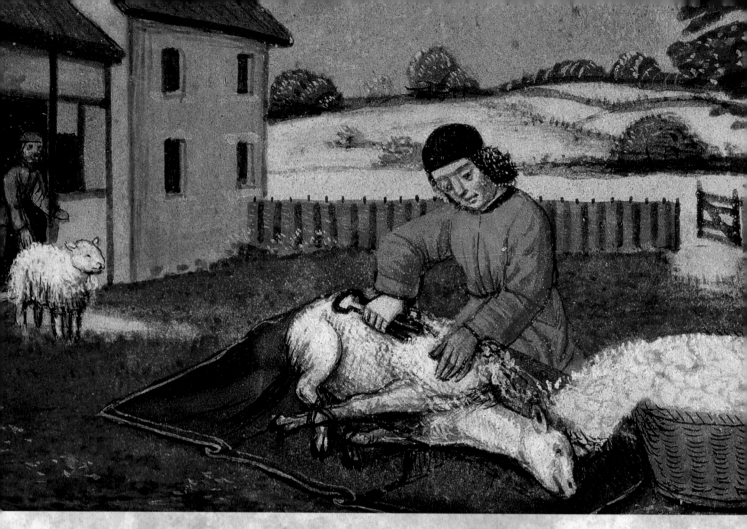

Beyond the Walls

Many castles were surrounded by fields where peasants grew crops for their lord. The peasants lived in villages, which usually had a church, a well, a mill, and a bakehouse with ovens.

Villagers' houses were made of wattle and daub. Wattle was a wooden frame filled with woven twigs. Daub was clay mixed with straw and dung. Roofs were made of straw, and floors were made of dirt. If the house had windows, they were very small, and there were shutters but no glass. A **hearth** in the middle of the floor provided warmth and a place to cook. Village homes had little furniture, and no indoor bathrooms.

▲ *A villager shears a sheep outside a home made of wattle and daub. Many of the peasants' clothes were made from wool, which the women spun and wove into cloth.*

▲ Peasants had to pay the lord grain or flour to use the lord's mill.

▼ Sometimes, a castle was built within the walls of a town or city, as in the medieval city of Carcassonne, in France. Concentric walls surround the city's castle, narrow streets, shops, and homes where people still live.

Growing Towns

Towns and cities grew around castles. A high wall protected the castle, and another high wall protected the town or city. Churches, marketplaces, bathhouses, where people paid to bathe before the days of indoor plumbing, and taverns and inns were inside the town walls.

Craftworkers, such as carpenters and shoemakers, lived and worked in towns and cities. Living near castles was a good way to earn money, since castles always needed supplies and workers. People near castles also felt safe, since they could retreat to the castle if they were attacked by enemies.

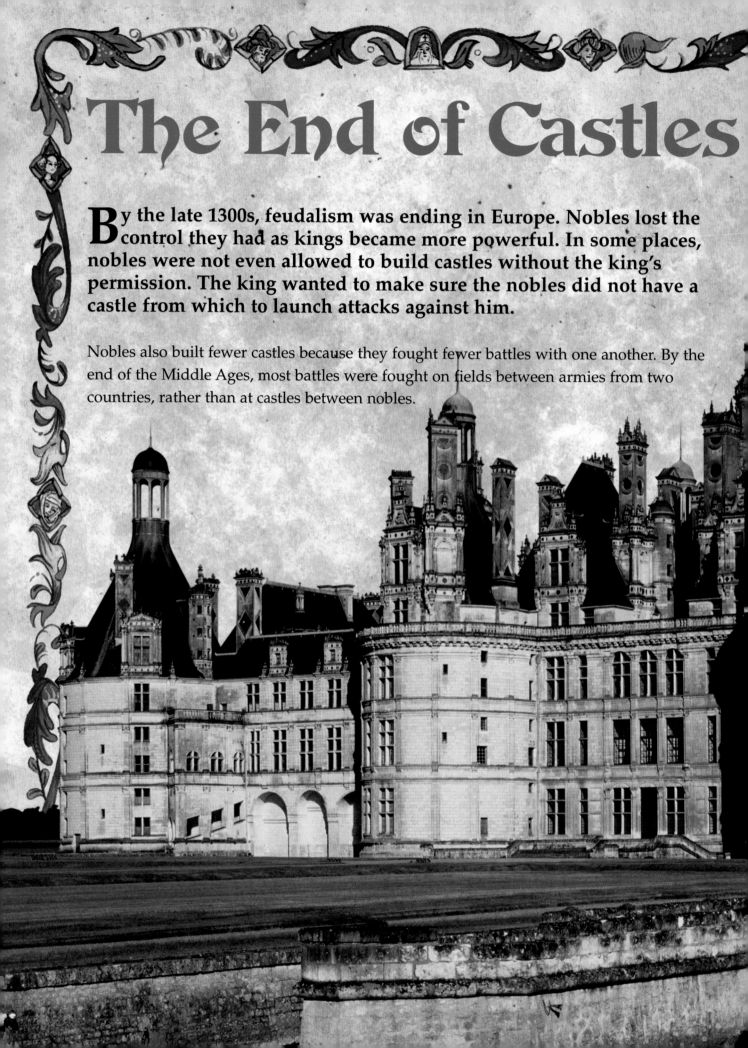

The End of Castles

By the late 1300s, feudalism was ending in Europe. Nobles lost the control they had as kings became more powerful. In some places, nobles were not even allowed to build castles without the king's permission. The king wanted to make sure the nobles did not have a castle from which to launch attacks against him.

Nobles also built fewer castles because they fought fewer battles with one another. By the end of the Middle Ages, most battles were fought on fields between armies from two countries, rather than at castles between nobles.

Later Castles

Many castles fell into ruin or were destroyed during wars. In the following centuries, people used the stone from ruined castles to build new homes. Other castles were turned into large houses that passed from one generation to the next. Over the last hundred years, many owners were forced to sell their castles because they were too expensive to heat and staff with servants. Today, many castles are hotels or museums that show what life was like in the Middle Ages.

Castles for Show

Starting around 1400, kings and other wealthy men built homes that looked like castles, but they were often only for show. These castles had few, if any, features that helped protect against enemy attacks. Most castles did not even have defensive walls. Instead, they were surrounded by gardens and fountains.

▼ *More than 1,800 people helped build the French castle of Chambord in the 1500s. It has 440 rooms, 365 fireplaces, and stables for 1,200 horses.*

Forts of the World

During the Middle Ages, people from outside Europe also built castles and large forts in their lands and in the lands they conquered. Many of these castles and forts still stand today.

Himeji Castle, Japan ▶

From around 1000 A.D, great warrior families in Japan fought with one another for land and power. They lived in castles, such as Himeji Castle, which was constructed in the 1300s and rebuilt in the 1600s.

Himeji Castle contains more than 80 buildings. The main keep, called the *tenshukaku*, is in the center of the castle. It has six stories, with five **projecting** roofs. From the *tenshukaku*, the castle residents watched for enemies. The *tenshukaku* was also a storeroom for weapons and the place to which everyone retreated when the castle was attacked.

◀ Daulatabad Fort, India

Daulatabad Fort is on top of a steep hill in western India. The original fort, called Deogiri, was built in the 800s. In the early 1100s, many features were added to improve the castle's defense, including several sets of thick walls, heavy iron gates with spikes that prevented elephants from ramming the gates open, and a deep moat filled with crocodiles. The hill on which the fort stood contained escape routes, secret passages, and traps.

In the 1300s, the sultan, or ruler, of the city of Delhi was so impressed by this fort that he moved his capital there. He renamed it Daulatabad, which means "the City of Fortune."

▲ Saladin's Citadel, Egypt

The Muslim leader Saladin built a citadel, or fort, in Egypt's capital city of Cairo between 1176 and 1183. The citadel's walls, which are 3,600 feet (1,200 meters) long, have small semicircular towers every 300 feet (100 meters), and several fortified gates. Later rulers added other features that helped protect the castle, including five large square keeps and two circular towers. The citadel also has a **mosque**, a palace, and a well.

Alhambra, Spain ▶

The Alhambra is a Muslim castle in Granada, Spain. It was constructed mainly between 1238 and 1358 to defend the city against Spanish Christians. The Christians had been fighting the Muslims, who were from North Africa, since they invaded Spain in 711.

Inside the Alhambra was a palace where the Muslim ruler of Granada lived. The palace was decorated with columns, arches, and beautifully painted tiles and woodwork. The Alhambra also had stables, baths, mosques, workshops, gardens, fountains, and courtyards. The Court of the Lions is a courtyard named after the fountain in its center which is surrounded by stone lions.

Glossary

ale A weak alcoholic drink made from grains

almoner A person who gives charity to the poor

battering ram A large weapon used to bash in castle gates

Byzantine Relating to an empire, once located in what is now Greece and Turkey

catapult A machine used to fling rocks and other weapons over castle walls

Christian Belonging to the religion of Christianity. Christians believe in one God and follow the teachings of Jesus Christ

embroidered Decorated with a design made in thread

ferment To change the chemicals in a liquid by adding yeast

fortified Protected or strengthened against attacks

foundation The supportive base of a building

game Wild animals killed for sport or food

garrison Soldiers who live permanently in a castle

hearth An open area surrounding a fire

invader A person who enters using force

lesser nobles Nobles who have less power or money than other nobles

machicolations Openings along castle walls through which defenders dropped stones

merchant A person who buys and sells goods

Middle East A region of the world that is now southwest Asia and northern Africa

minstrel A traveling musician and singer

moat A deep, wide ditch, often filled with water, that surrounds a castle for protection

mosque A sacred building in which Muslims worship

Muslim A person who believes in Islam, a religion based on the teachings of God, whom Muslims call Allah, and his prophet Muhammad

mutton The meat of an adult sheep

plumber A person who works with lead

preserved Food that has been bottled or salted to prevent it from spoiling

projecting Sticking out from the main building

survey To measure the shape and size of land

tax Money paid to nobles in exchange for land and protection

trestle A wooden base that supports a table

Index

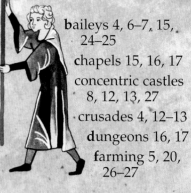

2 3 4 5 6 7 8 9 0   Printed in the U.S.A.   8 7 6 5